A Pennsylvania Bison Hunt

JACOB QUIGGLE, 1821–1911,*
ex-commissioner of Clinton County, grandson of
Philip Quigley,** early Pennsylvania buffalo hunter.

* Jacob S. Quiggle is buried in the Quiggle Cemetery near Lock Haven. He was the son of George Quiggle Sr. (1775-1843) and Catherine Strayer Quiggle (1794-1878). He may be a brother of James W. Quiggle (1820-1878), who is buried at the same place. James is the grandfather of the author, making Jacob a great uncle to Henry Wharton Shoemaker.

** Philip Quiggle, also buried in the Quiggle Cemetery, lived from 1745 to 1800. He was a Revolutionary War veteran, serving as an Ensign in the Cumberland County, Pennsylvania Associators and Militia under Colonel Samuel Lamb and Captain John Hamilton. He married Betsey Gilfillan circa 1770. Philip and Betsey would be the great-great-grandparents of Henry Wharton Shoemaker.

A PENNSYLVANIA BISON HUNT

Being the results of an investigation into the causes and period of the destruction of these noble beasts in the Keystone State, obtained from descendants of the original hunters. Including a sketch of the career of Daniel Ott. A Pennsylvanian who has killed many buffalo in the West.

HENRY W. SHOEMAKER

(Author of *Pennsylvania Deer and Their Horns*)

an imprint of Sunbury Press, Inc.
Mechanicsburg, PA USA

CATAMOUNT PRESS

an imprint of Sunbury Press, Inc.
Mechanicsburg, PA USA

Original Text Copyright © 1915, Henry W. Shoemaker.
Foreword and notations Copyright © 2026, Lawrence Knorr.
Cover Copyright © 2026 by Sunbury Press, Inc.

Sunbury Press supports copyright. Copyright fuels creativity, encourages diverse voices, promotes free speech, and creates a vibrant culture. Thank you for buying an authorized edition of this book and for complying with copyright laws. Except for the quotation of short passages for the purpose of criticism and review, no part of this publication may be reproduced, scanned, or distributed in any form without permission. You are supporting writers and allowing Sunbury Press to continue to publish books for every reader. For information contact Sunbury Press, Inc., Subsidiary Rights Dept., PO Box 548, Boiling Springs, PA 17007 USA or legal@sunburypress.com.

For information about special discounts for bulk purchases, please contact Sunbury Press Orders Dept. at (855) 338-8359 or orders@sunburypress.com.

To request one of our authors for speaking engagements or book signings, please contact Sunbury Press Publicity Dept. at publicity@sunburypress.com.

FIRST CATAMOUNT PRESS EDITION: January 2026

Set in Adobe Garamond | Interior design by Crystal Devine | Cover by Lawrence Knorr | Edited by Lawrence Knorr.

Publisher's Cataloging-in-Publication Data
Names: Shoemaker, Henry W., author.
Title: A Pennsylvania bison hunt / Henry W. Shoemaker.
Description: First trade paperback edition. | Mechanicsburg, PA : Catamount Press, 2026.
Summary: Being the results of an investigation into the causes and period of the destruction of these noble beasts in the Keystone State, obtained from descendants of the original hunters. Including a sketch of the career of Daniel Ott. A Pennsylvanian who has killed many buffalo in the West.
Identifiers: ISBN : 979-8-88819-343-3 (paperback).
Subjects: SPORTS & RECREATION / Hunting | HISTORY / United States / State & Local / Middle Atlantic | BIOGRAPHY & AUTOBIOGRAPHY / Sports.

Designed in the USA
0 1 1 2 3 5 8 13 21 34 55

For the Love of Books!

"Perhaps the most gigantic task ever undertaken on this continent in the line of game slaughter was the extermination of the bison. Probably the brilliant rapidity and success with which that lofty undertaking was accomplished was a matter of surprise even to those who participated in it. The story of the slaughter is by no means a long one."

—Dr. W. T. Hornaday[*]

---

[*] William Temple Hornaday (December 1, 1854 – March 6, 1937) was an American zoologist, conservationist, taxidermist, and author. He served as the first director of the New York Zoological Park, known today as the Bronx Zoo, and he was a pioneer in the early wildlife conservation movement in the United States. (Wikipedia)

TO DR. W. T. HORNADAY. SC. D.,
Who, more than any other man in America, has saved the bison from extinction, these pages are respectfully dedicated.

CONTENTS

Foreword xi
Introduction 1

    I.   Definitely Located 5
   II.   Description 9
  III.   The Passing 12
  IV.   The Last Stand 17
   V.   Last of His Race 24
  VI.   Re-Introduction 30
 VII.   Daniel Ott 36

Index 44

ILLUSTRATIONS

Jacob Quiggle, 1821 – 1911 . . . . . . (Frontispiece)
"Where the Vanished Millions Trod" 4
Grave of Col. John Kelly 26
Col. Kelly Homestead 27
Looking Down the Buffalo Path 33
Daniel Ott. 38

FOREWORD

HERE we are again, thinking about the work of Henry Wharton Shoemaker, whom I have dubbed "The Mark Twain of Pennsylvania." This particular volume, *A Pennsylvania Bison Hunt*, is often quoted and has been in demand since it was published in 1915. Many people believe the bison was prevalent in Pennsylvania up until the early 1800s based on Shoemaker's accounts. Shoemaker even invented his own variety of bison to explain their existence in the Keystone State. Unfortunately, this mysterious subspecies of these iconic creatures has yet to be confirmed in the fossil record or in any definitive way outside the Henry Wharton Shoemaker himself.

Some point to the account of Colonel John Kelly, the Revolutionary War hero, as the killer of the last bison in the Susquehanna Valley, circa 1801. Shoemaker credits the tale to Michael Grove, but does not cite the source from which he pulled the tale. Grove died about fifty years before Shoemaker was born, and was the brother of a legendary figure. The subsequent story of Kelly "offing" the Indian named Bull Head is also likely fanciful. It is most likely Colonel Kelly is best remembered for his service in the Revolution, especially at Princeton.

The tale of the McClellan cabin being inundated by bison who trampled the inhabitants before the men tore down the structure in a heroic rescue is typical Shoemaker legendry. The story is similar to his tale of dozens of wolves throwing themselves into a cabin to eliminate the pioneers within. If you are prone to believe it as fact, this author has some swampland near Karoondinha for sale!

Regardless, please enjoy this new, annotated edition of Henry Wharton Shoemaker's treatise on the Pennsylvania Bison. It is perhaps a lament at a time when it was realized how many of the great beasts had been lost in the West in the decades prior. While the science is mostly lacking, Shoemaker's heart was in the right place regarding his desire to see the species reintroduced. And, yes, you can sometimes see bison on farms around Pennsylvania. Just not the variety Shoemaker invented.

Lawrence Knorr, Ph.D.
January 2026

INTRODUCTION

WHEN a supposedly authoritative publication like "Report of the Pennsylvania Department of Agriculture for 1896" states that "perhaps two hundred years ago the lordly bison inhabited what is now the Keystone State," it would seem well-nigh impossible to trace down the animal's existence within our borders to a more comparatively recent date. The published references to the buffalo in Pennsylvania are few and far between. The earliest travelers and chroniclers, like Peter Kalm,[1] Dr. Schoepf,[2] and even William Penn, make little mention of them, but that is entirely due to the fact that in their travels they passed just outside

---

1. Pehr Kalm (6 March 1716 – 16 November 1779), also known as Peter Kalm, was a Swedish-Finnish explorer, botanist, naturalist, and agricultural economist. He was one of the most important apostles of Carl Linnaeus. (Wikipedia)

2. Johann David Schoepff, or Schoepf, or Schöpf, (8 March 1752 – 10 September 1800) was a German botanist, zoologist, and physician. (Wikipedia)

of the bison's limited range, although Albert Gallatin[3] has much to say concerning them.

Dr. W. T. Hornaday, in his monograph on the extermination of the American Bison, has devoted more space to the existence of these animals in the state than any other writer. In the map which he prepared showing the former range of the buffalo in North America, he has drawn a line approximately just west of the Susquehanna showing where the herds and then the stragglers lingered until the last years of the eighteenth century. This would bring the range a trifle west of Harrisburg, of Liverpool, of Sunbury, Lewisburg, Lock Haven, Emporium, and Bradford. West of that, the buffalo's range extended unbrokenly to the Rocky Mountains.

S. N. Rhoads,[4] in his *Mammals of Pennsylvania and New Jersey*, has furnished some interesting information on the bison in Pennsylvania, as has Professor J. A. Allen[5] in his very complete treatise. But they have failed to give anything like a description of the Pennsylvania Bison, how he looked, his size, habits, or the details of his extermination. With meagre records, the hunt for traces of the Bison of the Keystone State might seem discouraging, were it not for the wealth of oral traditions, embracing every topic connected with life in colonial days, which still runs like an underground stream through the hearts and minds of the old pioneers.[6]

These people, with their clear intellects, well-developed consciences, and kindly natures, are fast falling beneath the hand of the Reaper, but from them some record of the Pennsylvania Bison has been obtained, and on the following pages is preserved. However, much of what has been thus obtained will only interest the scientist and the student, for

---

3. Abraham Alfonse Albert Gallatin (January 29, 1761 – August 12, 1849) was a Genevan-American politician, diplomat, ethnologist, and linguist. (Wikipedia)

4. Samuel Nicholson Rhoads (1862-1952) was an ornithologist. His papers are kept at the Historical Society of Haddonfield, New Jersey. He is buried at the Haddonfield Friends Meeting Cemetery in that town. His book *The Mammals of Pennsylvania and New Jersey* was self-published in Philadelphia in 1903.

5. Joel Asaph Allen (July 19, 1838 – August 29, 1921) was an American zoologist, mammalogist, and ornithologist. He became the first president of the American Ornithologists' Union, the first curator of birds and mammals at the American Museum of Natural History, and the first head of that museum's Department of Ornithology. (Wikipedia)

6. Samuel N. Rhoads, "Distribution of the American Bison in Pennsylvania, with Remarks on a New Fossil Species," published in Proceedings of the Academy of Natural Sciences of Philadelphia, 1895, Volume 47, pp. 244-248, states "Regarding the question of the existence of B. bison in the valleys of eastern Pennsylvania since the advent of the white man in America, it is probable that it had been effectually driven from the Delaware Valley long before that date. Indeed, from the scarcity of its remains and the absence of reliable tradition of its presence in this locality, it is unlikely that this species was ever more than a straggler in the regions east of the Susquehanna River drainage."

it matters little to most persons to learn that the Pennsylvania bison was different in appearance from most of his western congeners, that he belonged to the type known as the *wood bison*.

At the same time, it does seem worthwhile to present a description of our bison from the lips of the grandson of a noted hunter of the species. It brings us closer to this vanished forest monarch, makes *Bison americanus* seem more real. But from points of difference, he deserves to be called *Bison americanus Pennsylvanicus*.[7] Doubtless, west of the Alleghenies, the individuals shaded into the true bison of the plains, but those which ranged between the east and west slopes of the Alleghenies, migrating between the Great Lakes, and the valleys of southern Pennsylvania, Maryland, and Virginia, to Georgia, represented the type of bison of the Keystone State. Presumably, in Georgia, they encountered the northern migrations of a southern or southwestern type of bison, the bison of Louisiana, but probably it too was closely related to the Pennsylvania type. The lengthy migrations were hardly in keeping with known characteristics of the wood bison of Colorado, Wyoming, and Montana, and of the Canadian Northwest. But this can be clearly judged and determined after the stated facts are weighed and digested. Most interesting of all seems the vast numbers of bison which roamed through the central and western parts of our state, now gone and forgotten through man's rapacious greed.

---

7. This designation is an invention of the author.

"WHERE THE VANISHED MILLIONS TROD." (With Portrait of Mr. J. W. Zimmerman.*)

* Jacob Wren Zimmerman (1853-1940) was buried at Mount Union Cemetery in Carroll, Clinton County, Pennsylvania. He was the son of David A. Zimmerman and Mary Wren. He was a lumberman who worked for Ario Pardee in the White Deer Valley. He was known as a great hunter and fisherman and was widely known as fiddler for mountain dances and a singer of old ballads.

I.

DEFINITELY LOCATED

IT was early in August 1911 that a "clam bake" was given at Quiggle Springs, near McElhattan in Clinton County. Though the bake was far from a success, as those present well remember, the information concerning the bison in Pennsylvania gleaned from it made it a memorable occasion. About nine o'clock in the evening, while waiting for the clams to be served, the moon began to rise from behind the Bald Eagle Mountain, which towered above the park. The conversation had turned to old Hyloshotkee,[8] the Cayuga chief who once resided at the Five Springs, to the eloquent Logan[9] who often camped there, and then drifted to the subject of hunting adventures.

---

8. Hyloshotkee, "a peaceful chief living at McElhattan Springs," mentioned in several Shoemaker tales. He is most likely not a historical figure. He is not mentioned in any other sources.

9. Logan the Orator (c. 1723 – 1780) was a Cayuga orator and war leader born of one of the Six Nations of the Haudenosaunee Confederacy. (Wikipedia) He was a son of Shikellamy. However, it is unlikely Logan camped at McElhattan for any period.

One of the guests, Jacob Quiggle,[10] formerly a Commissioner of Clinton County, at that time nearing his ninetieth birthday, remarked that he had often heard of Hyloshotkee's prowess as a buffalo hunter. Immediately, the writer's curiosity was aroused—he had previously interrogated the aged gentleman on almost every other subject of Pennsylvania antiquity—and now he was to learn something definite about the bison. Mr. Quiggle's keen gray eyes kindled with interest in the subject, and he went on to say that his grandfather, Philip Quigley or Quiggle, who settled in what is now Wayne Township, Clinton County, in 1773, and later was an officer in the Revolutionary War, had been known far and wide as a buffalo hunter.

He had been born in Cumberland County in 1745 and grew to manhood with the buffalo just across the Blue Ridge from his home. As they were gradually driven west and north, to Buffalo Creek in Bedford County, to Buffalo Valley in Union County, he had followed them, until finding a spot of ground which suited him on the West Branch, he had settled in the heart of the Indian and big game country. The famous "Buffalo Path" had run within a few rods of his cabin, extending through the valley of Henry Run, to the east end of Sugar Valley, thence across the Red Hills, through the west end of White Deer Valley, across the Buffalo Mountains, into Buffalo Valley, across that valley, over Jack's and the White Mountains, into Middle Creek Valley where the giant beasts wintered in countless numbers. Earlier, they had continued their migrations probably as far as Georgia, many bison crossing from the Ohio country into southern Pennsylvania via Clearfield.[11]

Thomas Ashe,[12] in his *Travels in America in 1806* says: "The best roads to the Onondaga from all parts are the buffalo-tracks; so called

---

10. Jacob Quiggle died two months later, on October 16, 1911.

11. Note that there remains no fossil record of bison in this area.

12. Thomas Ashe (1770–1835), novelist and travel writer, was born 15 July 1770 in Glasnevin, Co. Dublin, third son among eleven children of Jonathan Ashe, soldier, and Margaret Ashe (née Hickman), heiress to estates in Co. Clare. According to his own account, he spent his early life at Ashville, near Limerick, and was educated in Clonmel, Co. Tipperary. After serving in the British army, he entered the wine trade in Bordeaux, where he was briefly imprisoned for wounding the brother of a girl he had seduced. He returned to Dublin and through the recommendations of his eldest brother, Jonathan, was appointed secretary to the Diocesan and Endowed Schools Commission. However, he enjoyed himself 'in a total disregard to official duties'; and, in debt, resigned and spent several years travelling in Europe and America, where he continued to live a 'chequered and adventurous life'. The details of a life, perhaps too full of incident and escapade to be credible, are described in colourful prose in Memoirs and confessions (1815) and several other books, including Memoirs of mammoth and other bones (1806) and A commercial and geographical sketch of Brazil and Madeira (1812). Of his work Travels in America in 1806 (1808), the critic

from having been observed to be made by the buffaloes in their annual visitations to the lake from their pasture-grounds; and though this is a distance of above two hundred miles, the best surveyor could not have chosen a more direct course, or firmer or better ground. I have often traveled these tracks with safety and admiration; I perceived them chosen as if by the nicest judgment; and when at times I was perplexed to find them revert on themselves nearly in parallel lines, I soon found it occasioned by swamps, ponds, or precipices, which the animals knew how to avoid; but that object being affected, the road again swept into its due course, and bore towards its destination as if under the direction of a compass."

Reverend John Ettwein,[13] in his *Notes of Travel in 1772,* says, "Reached Clearfield Creek, where the buffaloes formerly cleared large tracts of undergrowth, so as to give them the appearance of cleared fields; hence the Indians call the creek Clearfield." The herds had been cut in two by the settlers in Philip Quigley's time; the northern and western herds could move no further south than the Valley of Middle Creek. Those in the south had to remain there.

Mr. Quiggle stated that when the persimmons became ripe along the Bald Eagle Mountains, it was time to look for southern migrations of the buffalo. In a single file, they crossed the Susquehanna River just below the Great Island, a short distance east of Lock Haven, followed approximately the line of the New York Central Railroad easterly through Wayne Township, and thence south through the gap in the Bald Eagle Mountains, made by the waters of Henry Run, formerly called Love Run. In Penn's and Middle Creek Valley, they were joined by herds that came from the western part of the state via Clearfield.

When the red bud was in bloom, it was time to look for the northerly migration. In the autumn migrations, they were mostly killed for their hides, but in spring, mainly calves were killed, as buffalo calf meat was highly relished by the pioneers. The calves were born from March to July.

---

in the London Quarterly Review wrote: 'He has spoiled a good book by engrafting incredible stories on authentic facts.' (Dictionary of Irish Biography)

13. John Ettwein (1721–1802), a native of Germany, came to America in 1754 to undertake missionary work among the Indians. Initially an open Loyalist, he was imprisoned briefly before concluding that the church should not take a public stand on American independence. Stationed at Bethlehem, he acted as chaplain at the American hospital there and represented the Moravians in negotiations with Congress and the Pennsylvania legislature about their refusal to enlist in the army or subscribe to the test oath. In 1784, Ettwein became bishop of the Moravian Church in America. (National Archives)

When the settlers harassed the buffalo, they tried to migrate at night as much as possible, and at the Great Island crossing, they split into three streams, one pouring through Castanea Gap, to the head of the Kammerdiner Run, and following it east to where it joins with McElhattan Run, to connect with the file which went through McElhattan Gap.[14] Thence these two files went out of the valley of Spring Run, where they joined the file that had come through the Henry Run Gap. The bison traveled not only with order but with time, as they came together like clockwork, as if by preconceived orders, at the head of Spring Run.

---

14. Of course, the bison would file right by the McElhattan Estate!

II.

DESCRIPTION

ASKED definitely to describe the Pennsylvania bison, Mr. Quiggle stated that his memory was clear on that point, for although his grandfather, the hunter, had died before his birth, and his father had passed on while he was still a young boy, from his mother and other older relatives, he had heard the subject gone over again and again. In the first place, the bison of Pennsylvania was a tremendous animal. Like the wood bison[15] of the flanks of the Rocky Mountains and Canada Northwest, he exceeded in size the buffalo met with west of Ohio, Kentucky, and Tennessee.

In color, the Pennsylvania bison was very dark, many of the old bulls being coal black, with grizzly white hairs around the nose and eyes. The hair was very short, with a tendency to crispness and curliness, especially at the joints. The hump, so conspicuous on the western bison, was

---

15. The wood bison prefers boreal (pine) forests in colder climes, found mostly in Canada.

notable by its absence. The first settlers, on seeing the animals, called them "wild bulls."[16]

The legs were long, and fore and back legs evenly placed; the heavy front and meager hindquarters of the western bison were not present; in other words, the Pennsylvania bison was a beautifully proportioned beast. He was an agile runner and climber, carried no superfluous flesh, and was adapted in every way for life in a rough, mountainous country. The bulls often weighed a ton, the mature cows half that much.

The hair on the neck and shoulders was no longer than on other parts of the body, except with mature bulls, who carried a sort of mane or crest which reached its maximum length where the hump grows on the prairie buffalo. Both males and females wore beards, but they were not heavy and consisted of tufts of straight, stiff black hair. The horns, which in mature specimens were very long, grew upwards, like the horns of Ayrshire cattle. Apparently, the horns were much like those of *Bison bonasus* of Lithuania and the Caucasus.

The Pennsylvania bison preferred dense forests, although on warm, sunshiny days in winter, they could be found sunning themselves in abandoned Indian fields in Middle Creek Valley. In early spring, they could be found pasturing along Lake Erie and Lake Ontario, but as the season advanced, they gradually retired to the cool mountain tops in northern Pennsylvania, where they lingered until the first snows—the "persimmon time"[17] further south. By the time of the fall migration, calves that had been born mostly in March and April were well advanced, and many appeared to be the size of yearling cattle.

The impression among the early hunters was that the great northern herd, which, when Philip Quigley settled on the West Branch in 1773, still numbered about 12,000 animals, was split up into a vast number of "families," consisting of a mature bull and a dozen cows with a like number of yearlings and calves. At the end of the migration followed the weaker and aged bulls, which had no mates, also the buffalo oxen of still greater size than the biggest bulls; these last-named castrated by the wolves of northern Pennsylvania.

Behind the stragglers skulked troops of gray wolves, which followed the herd as far as the Great Island crossing, where they retired, the pursuit

---

16. They were most likely referring to bull elk.
17. Pennsylvania persimmons peak in October.

being taken up by packs of smaller brown wolves, which followed the bison from the famous wolf rocks on Henry Run as far south as White Deer Valley, where they retired in favor of the larger black wolves. These black wolves, whose stronghold was in the Seven Mountains, preyed on the sickly, wounded, and aged buffalo during their entire winter's stay in the Valley of Middle Creek.

III.

THE PASSING

ON the northerly migrations, according to Mr. Quiggle, bands of buffalo were constantly dropping out of the great herd; these were the "families," each led by a giant bull. Many of these groups summered in the high tablelands of the Seven Mountains, in what is now Gregg Township, Centre County, where they seemed to feel particularly content. By 1770, no bison summered in the ridges adjacent to the West Branch Valley, as the settlers kept them on the run; even at migration time, they would have avoided crossing the valley had not the instinct of countless centuries been too difficult to overcome.

When the part of the herd which once summered at the northern limit of the range, which was where the city of Buffalo, New York, now stands, commenced their southern journey, in some mysterious way, probably by an acute sense of smell, knowledge of this was imparted to the heads of the bison families which had "dropped off" at each sequestered and grassy spot on the way north in the spring. These heads of families would ascend to the tops of high peaks and bellow loudly for several days, drawing their little colonies around them, and when the herd passed down the path, they would fall into line for the journey to the southland. This bellowing, or drawing together of the clans, informed the hunters of the migration's proximity, and all they had to do was post themselves along the paths and kill as many bison as they wished. Many were killed for sport or to prevent the settlers further south from enjoying them.

These buffalo paths, which all converged with the main path, were often worn two feet deep with the tread of the countless herds for countless years. The bark of the adjacent trees had all worn off from the huge creatures rubbing themselves. Along Buffalo Path Run, in Buffalo Gap, Union County, the path is very plainly marked today, although no buffalo have tramped over it in a hundred and fifteen years! Until it was cut some years ago, a large hemlock tree by this path showed the marks where it had been rubbed by the bison. The path is a familiar landmark, and part of it is a trail to this day for prospectors, hunters, fishermen, and berry-pickers.

Although the Indians of Pennsylvania killed many buffalo, they only did so for food and clothing, and were careful to keep alive plenty of good, healthy breeders. They only killed such animals as were necessary to them; not a single bone or sinew was wasted. With such hunting, there was no danger of buffalo or any other animals becoming extinct.

It was only when the white hunters came, men of lowly origin, whose forebears were not allowed to carry firearms or enter the game preserves and parks of the gentry of the old country, who slaughtered the bison without rhyme or reason. They killed for the sheer love of gore and brutality; they killed until ammunition and strength became exhausted; they killed lest somebody else later on have something left to kill.

In Pennsylvania, these rapacious beings speedily wiped out the tens of thousands of buffalo, as well as the moose, elk, brown bears, beavers, otters, fishers, heath cocks, paroquets, pileated woodpeckers, wild pigeons, and other valuable and necessary animals and birds. It is a horrible story to relate, but it is not ended, as the descendants of these *gauche* marauders have ravaged and burned forests, and now their factories pollute our rivers and streams and kill the fish. They will not be content until Pennsylvania is as desolate as China, and they have prevented posterity from having anything worthwhile!

Gradually, the herds that headed south became fewer and fewer in number. The aggregation, which passed through Henry Run annually, undoubtedly joined a still larger body in Middle Creek Valley in an early day on their march to Georgia. But towards the end, the Valley of Middle Creek was as far south as they dared to travel, and some of the vast armies from western Pennsylvania came to join them no more.

In various parts of the state, we get glimpses of how plentiful the bison were at the end of the eighteenth century. Professor Allen quotes from Thomas Ashe's well-known book, *Travels in America in 1806*, as follows: "In the vicinity of the spot where the town of Clarion now stands, in northwestern Pennsylvania, one of the first settlers built a log cabin near a salt spring which was visited by buffaloes in such numbers that he supposed there could not have been less than two thousand there at a time."[18] Professor Allen stated that near the heads of Oil Creek and the Clarion River, there were, at one time, thousands of buffalo.

Waterford, in Erie County, was originally called Le Boeuf[19] and is situated on Le Boeuf Lake. French Creek in Venango County was originally Riviere des Boeufs. Big Buffalo Creek is in Armstrong County, all famous resorts of the bison in the old days. They were more prevalent in Pennsylvania than all the vast herds of various wild animals that were found by the first pioneers in south and south-central Africa.

S. N. Rhoads further quotes Ashe as saying that the old settler at Clarion declared that for the first several seasons the buffaloes visited his salt spring with the utmost regularity. They traveled in single file, always following each other at equal distances, forming droves on their arrival of about three hundred each. These embraced probably a score of family groups, which perhaps had some "clan" relationship. The first and second years, so unacquainted were these poor brutes with this man's house or with his nature, that in a few hours they rubbed the house completely down,

---

18. The veracity of Ashe's account is in question.
19. Le Beouf means beef or cattle in French.

taking delight in turning the logs of wood off with their horns, while he had some difficulty to escape from being trampled under their feet or crushed to death in his own ruins. At that time, he estimated there could not have been less than ten thousand in the neighborhood of the spring.

They sought for no manner of food but only bathed and drank three or four times a day and rolled in the earth, or reposed with their flanks distended, in the adjacent shades, and departed in single files, according to the exact order of their arrival. They all rolled successively in the same hole, and each thus carried away a coat of mud to preserve the moisture of the skin, which, when hardened and baked by the sun, would resist the stings of millions of insects that otherwise would persecute these peaceful travelers to madness or even death.

In the first and second years this old man with some companions killed from six to seven hundred of these noble creatures, merely for the sake of the skins, which to them were worth only two shillings each, and after this "work of death" they were obliged to leave the place 'til the following season, or 'til the wolves, bears, panthers, eagles, rooks, ravens, etc., had devoured the carcasses and abandoned the place for other prey.

In the two following years the same persons killed great numbers out of the first droves that arrived, skinned them and left the bodies exposed to the sun and air; but the soon had reason to repent of this; for the remaining droves, as they came up in succession, stopped, gazed on the mangled and putrid bodies, sorrowfully moaned or furiously lowed aloud, and returned instantly to the wilderness in an unusual run without tasting their favorite spring or licking the impregnated earth, which was also once their most agreeable occupation; nor did they or any of their race ever revisit that neighborhood.

There was a salt spring in Dauphin County that the bison visited in spring and fall. It was situated in the wilds of the Stony Creek Country, and the vast herds to reach it crossed the river at Haldeman's Island, near the mouth of the Juniata. Many were drowned at high water, so intent were they to reach their favorite retreat. Thomas Ashe says, elsewhere in his book, referring to the bloody scenes at Clarion, "The simple history of this spring is that of every other in the settled parts of this western world. I met with a man who had killed two thousand buffaloes (in

Pennsylvania) with his own hand, and others no doubt have done the same thing. In consequence of this proceeding, not one buffalo is at this time (1811) found east of the Mississippi, except a few domesticated by the curious or carried through the country on a public show."[20]

John Filson,[21] writing in 1784 of the Blue Licks in Kentucky, stated, "I have heard a hunter assert he saw about one thousand buffaloes at these licks at once; so numerous were they before the first settlers had wantonly sported away their lives."

All through Pennsylvania, the story was the same: wanton, sordid, and unnecessary, the annihilation of a race of animals which could have been domesticated and furnished hides and beef to a vast population. Perhaps it is just as well that so few of the details of the Pennsylvania bison are available, as they would sicken and disgust all thoughtful and sensible persons. It is best that the waters of oblivion have closed over the entire horrible transaction, yet a word to the wise is sometimes sufficient to stay the hand that is bent on wiping out the remaining forms of wild life in the Keystone State. The passing of our bison should serve as an object lesson of the need of organized conservation, if our deer, bears, wild cats, wild turkeys, and grouse are to be saved.

Thomas Ashe, in commenting on the cruel annihilation of the lordly bison, says: "The first settlers, not content with this sanguinary extermination of the animals, also destroyed the food to which it was most partial, which was the cane, growing in forests and brakes of immeasurable extent. To this, the unsparing wretches set fire in dry seasons; to drive out every living creature and then hunt and persecute them to death."

---

20. Thomas Ashe traveled in 1806 and could not have made such an observation in 1811, five years into the future. Clarion is not mentioned in Ashe's book. Shoemaker is either inventing this statement or is mistaken as to the source.

21. John Filson (c. 1747 – October 1788) was an American author, historian of Kentucky, pioneer, surveyor and one of the founders of Cincinnati, Ohio. (Wikipedia)

IV.

THE LAST STAND

OLD Flavel Bergstresser[22] was for several years a familiar figure about the ancient Kleckner House at New Berlin. The former seat of justice of Union County lies immediately east of the White Mountains, where the bison made their last stand in Pennsylvania. The aged man, who picked up an honest penny by hosteling and doing chores for traveling men, was a genial soul, and on occasion could be induced to tell of his illustrious family connections. Chief among his celebrated forbears was his great-grandfather, Martin Bergstresser,[23] a Snyder County pioneer, who helped to wipe out the last herd of wild bison in the Keystone State.

Incidentally, through marriage, he was related to Flavel Roan,[24] an eccentric genius who in his youth had been famed as a slayer of Pennsylvania

---

22. This individual could not be located.
23. This individual may be fictional.
24. Linn's Annals of Buffalo Valley (pg. 439) says, "February 19, Flavel Roan, Esquire, born July 31, 1760. Son of the Reverend John Roan, and brother of Mrs. Clingan. He was buried in the Presbyterian graveyard, at Lewisburg, near the pavement, a little east of the present church. The grave being unmarked, it was lost sight of when the church was built."

bison. About twelve years ago, when the writer was in Union and Snyder Counties, gathering the old folktales and legends of the Pennsylvania mountains, he was directed to Flavel Bergstresser as the possessor of a retentive memory and a seemingly inexhaustible stock of information.

It happened that one of the writer's companions on the excursion was Captain John Q. Dyce,[25] of Clinton County, famed in central Pennsylvania as a poet, orator, and student of folklore. Captain Dyce and Bergstresser recognized one another as old friends, as they had gone through Muncy Dam together on a raft, which followed the one that was wrecked, causing the loss of three young men on a memorable May morning in 1843. One tale of the long ago led to another, old Bergstresser waxing eloquent when he realized that he was being treated as an equal and a man of intelligence and not as a broken-down hostler, to be sworn at and kicked about. The conversation passed from rafting to politics, from politics to religion, from religion to hunting, where it stuck, for both old men were enthusiastic devotees of the chase.

It began with wild pigeons, passed to brown bears, to panthers, to elks, and then to buffaloes, to a time before the memory of most living Pennsylvanians. Sitting down in a comfortable corner of the steps of the hotel, and leaning against an upright, old Bergstresser took off his hat, stroked his long white beard, and related the story of the annihilation of the last bison herd and the last individual buffalo in Pennsylvania. The story is given in full in Chapter XVII of the writer's *More Pennsylvania Mountain Stories*, but the salient facts will be given in the ensuing paragraphs.

It appeared from what Bergstresser said, that by the close of the eighteenth century, the last herd of Pennsylvania bison, numbering nearly four hundred animals of all ages, had taken refuge in the wilds of the Seven Mountains. The settlements in Middle Creek Valley prevented them from wintering there as of yore, and the persistent slaughter in the West Branch Valley made it unsafe for them to try to escape to the north. Hemmed in on all sides, they survived a while by hiding on the highest and most inaccessible mountains, or in the deepest and darkest ravines.

The winter of 1799-1800 was particularly severe, and life on the bleak mountain tops became unbearable to the starving brutes. They

---

25. This individual may be fictional.

must penetrate into the valleys, where grass could be dug out from under the snow, or perish of hunger. Led by a giant coal black bull called "Old Logan," after the Mingo chieftain of that name, the herd started in single file one winter's morning for the clear and comfortable stretches of the Valley of Middle Creek. While passing through the woods at the edge of a clearing belonging to a young man named Samuel McClellan,[26] they were attacked by that nimrod, who killed four fine cows. Previously, while still on the mountain, a count of the herd had been made, and it numbered three hundred and forty-five animals. Passing from the McClellan property, the herd fell afoul of the barnyard and haystack of Martin Bergstresser, a settler who had recently arrived from Berks County. His first season's hay crop, a good-sized pile, stood beside his recently completed log barn. This hay was needed to feed for the winter to a number of cows and sheep, and a team of horses. The cattle and sheep were sidling close to the stack when they scented the approaching buffalo. With "Old Logan" at their head, the famished bison herd broke through the stump fence, crushing the helpless domestic animals beneath their mighty rush, and were soon complacently pulling to pieces the hay-pile.

Bergstresser, who was in a nearby field cutting wood, heard the commotion and rushed to the scene. Aided by his daughter Katie, a girl of eighteen, and Samuel McClellan, who joined the party, four buffalo were slain. The deaths of their comrades and the attacks of the settlers' dogs terrified the buffaloes, and they swept out of the barnyard and up the frozen bed of the creek. When they were gone, awful was the desolation left behind. The barn was still standing, but the fences, spring house, and haystack were gone, as if swept away by a flood. Six cows, four calves, and thirty-five sheep lay crushed and dead among the ruins. The horses which were inside the barn remained unharmed.

McClellan started homeward after the departure of the buffaloes, but when he got within sight of his clearing, he uttered a cry of surprise and horror. Three hundred or more bison were snorting and trotting around the lot where his cabin stood, obscuring the structure by their huge dark bodies. The pioneer rushed bravely through the roaring, crazy, surging mass, only to find "Old Logan," his eyes bloodshot and flaming, standing guard in front of the cabin door. He fired at the monster, wounding

---

26. Samuel McClellan (1776-1854) is buried at Buffalo Crossroads Presbyterian Cemetery in Union County, Pennsylvania.

him, which so further infuriated the giant bull that he plunged headlong through the door of the cabin. The herd, accustomed at all times to follow their leader, forced their way after him as best they could through the narrow opening. Vainly did McClellan fire his musket, and when the ammunition was exhausted, he drove his bear knife into the beasts' flanks to try and stop them in their mad course.

Inside were the pioneer's wife and three little children, the oldest five years, and he dreaded to think of their awful fate. He could not stop the buffalo, which continued filing through the doorway until they were jammed in the cabin as tightly as wooden animals in a toy Noah's ark. No sounds came from the victims inside; all he could hear was the snorting and bumping of the giant beasts in their cramped quarters.

The sound of the crazy stampede brought Martin Bergstresser and three other neighbors to the spot, all carrying guns. It was decided to tear down the cabin as the only possible means of saving the lives of the McClellan family. When the cabin had been battered down, the bison, headed by Old Logan, swarmed from the ruins like giant black bees from a hive. McClellan had the pleasure of shooting Old Logan as he emerged, but it was small satisfaction. When the men entered the cabin, they were shocked to find the bodies of the pioneer's wife and three children dead and crushed deep into the mud of the earthen floor by the cruel hoofs. Of the furniture, nothing remained of a larger size than a handspike.[27]

The news of this terrible tragedy spread all over the valley, and it was suggested on all sides that the murderous bison be completely exterminated. The idea took concrete form when Bergstresser and McClellan started, on horseback, one riding toward the river and the other toward the headwaters of Middle Creek, to invite the settlers to join the hunt. Meanwhile, there was another blizzard, but every man invited accepted with alacrity. About fifty hunters assembled at the Bergstresser home and marched like an invading army in the direction of the mountains. Among them were Jacob Stuck, George Ott, Emmanuel Snyder, Abraham Sourkill, George Schnable, John Young, William Doran, George Everhart, Gottfried Fryer, Jacob Fryer, Dennis Mucklehenny, Peter Fisher, Christian Fisher, John Hager, Jacob Long Sr., George Michael,

---

27. Clearly a fictional, sensational tale. Bison crowded in a cabin?

Francis Rhoads, Conrad Weiser Jr., Peter Arbogast, Joseph Pauling, Albert Swineford, John Swineford, George Swineford, Jacob Jarrett Sr., John Middleswarth, George Good, John Hittardantive, Harry Lauder, Harry Lehr, Jonathan Farnsworth, George Wickersham, George Weirick, John Hartman, Adam Dressler, George Kessler, John Kreigbaum, George Benfer, John Hummel, Solomon Miller, Moses Troup, Peter Troup.

After all these years, some of the names have a strangely familiar ring. Many dogs, some partly wolf, accompanied the hunters. They were out two days before discovering their quarry, as the fresh snow had covered all the buffalo paths. The brutes were all huddled together up to their necks in snow in a great hollow space known as the Sink formed by Boonestiel's Tongue in the heart of the White Mountains, near the present town of Weikert, Union County, and the hunters looking down on them from the high plateau above, now known as the Big Flats, estimated their number at three hundred.

When they got among the animals, they found them numb from cold and hunger, but had they been physically able, they could not have moved, so deeply were they crusted in the drifts. The work of slaughter quickly began. Some used guns, but the most killed them by cutting their throats with long bear knives. The snow was too deep to attempt skinning them, but many tongues were saved, and these the backwoodsmen shoved into the huge pockets of their deerskin coats until they could hold no more. After the last buffalo had been dispatched, the triumphant hunters climbed back to the summit of Council Kup, where they lit a huge bonfire which was to be a signal to the women and children in the valleys below that the last herd of Pennsylvania bison was no more, and that the McClellan family had been avenged. Then the party marched down to the lowlands singing German hymns.

It was a horrible sight that they left behind them in the Sink. Three hundred dead buffalo stood upright in the frozen crust, most with jaws broken and all with tongues gone, while the ice about them resembled a sheet of crimson glass. Later in the season, some of the hunters returned to see if they could procure a few of the hides, but the alternate freezes and thaws had rendered them valueless. To this day, the barren flat where the McClellan cabin stood is known as the Buffalo Field. It is situated on high ground a short distance to the east of the old distillery near Troxelville.

The date of the annihilation of the last bison herd is put by Bergstresser at December 31, 1799.[28] He comes to this conclusion as he has always heard it was "after Christmas and before the New Year." If there were other herds from the western part of the state wiped out at about this time or later, the writer has been unable to obtain an inkling. Most probably, they were driven into Ohio and West Virginia and were annihilated.

Dr. Schoepf, journeying from Harrisburg to Pittsburgh in 1783, states in his valuable book *Travels in the Confederation* that the buffalo in the vicinity of Pittsburgh had been driven to Ohio before he arrived in the future Smoky City. However, only a few years before, bison were found in large numbers on Buffalo Creek in Bedford County. The year 1795 marked the disappearance of the last herds from the northwestern part of the state, and the migrations from Lake Erie to southern Pennsylvania had ceased before the Great Runaway on the West Branch in 1778.

Doubtless, at one time, probably as late as 1770, the streams of bison from New York and the Ohio Country united in the southern Pennsylvania valleys and swarmed in solid phalanx into the warmer regions of the Carolinas and Tennessee each winter. Settlements in southern Pennsylvania checked the migrations, and no bison moved farther south than Middle Creek Valley after that. To come north meant death. The Seven Mountains became the final stronghold of the buffalo from the north and northwest of Pennsylvania. Gradually, these were killed off or perished from severe winters and lack of food. The herd killed at the close of 1799 was probably the last, except for a few stragglers remaining in the state.

If they had not blundered into the valley of Middle Creek, impelled by blind instinct and starvation, they might have lasted a score of years longer, or into the memory of men now living. Their extinction, therefore, was en masse and not gradual like the later extermination of the elk. This accident caused their wiping out, as they were otherwise as able to care for themselves than the elk. The elk traveled in herds, migrated between the northern mountains and southern Valleys in Pennsylvania,

---

28. Interesting that it is the last day of the century! So, the bison were definitely eradicated before 1800!

and were no more fleet of foot or shy than the buffalo. One by one, the elk were shot out, until the last met its end in the Black Gap, on October 1, 1878. From the point where Captain Daniel Engle slew the last native wild elk in Pennsylvania to where Colonel John Kelly killed the last known buffalo on February 19, 1801, is less than a dozen miles as the crow flies. These noble brutes met their end bravely amid the wild scenery they loved so well.

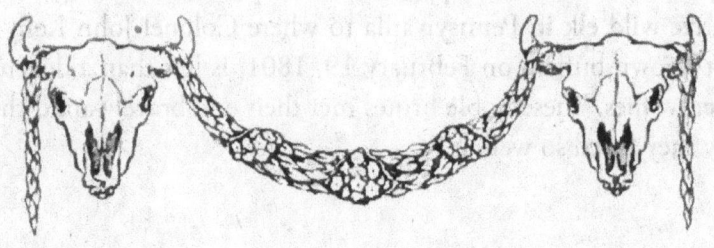

V.

LAST OF HIS RACE

COLONEL John Kelly, slayer of the last wild buffalo in Pennsylvania, was born within a stone's throw of the birthplace of Robert Fulton, in Lancaster County, on February 11, 1744. Little is known of his early career except that he chafed at the monotony of life in a settled country and longed for the "sweet dangers" of the frontier. In 1768, he removed to Buffalo Valley, which had long been noted as a feeding ground for vast herds of bison. Buffalo Creek, which flowed through the valley, was the favorite bathing place for the "vanished millions." Numbers of these noble brutes always summered on Buffalo Mountain.

Six feet tall, with sandy hair and blue eyes, John Kelly made an ideal pioneer. He never knew such a thing as fatigue or discouragement. He became a famous Indian fighter and is said to have had one hundred "nicks" on his trusty rifle, indicating the number of natives whom he made "bite the dust." Many anecdotes are told of his prowess in battling with the fierce savages. They are among the most thrilling in the annals of Indian warfare. When the Revolutionary War broke out, he was among the first to enlist for the colonists. Being rapidly promoted for bravery, he soon attained the rank of Colonel. His bravery at the Battle of Princeton was conspicuous. After the Revolution, he returned to his comfortable homestead in what is now Kelly Township, Union County.

There were still a few marauding Indians to kill, but he devoted his time principally to farming and hunting big game. His specialty was buffalo, and his friends stated that he killed over a hundred of these animals. The stories of some of his hunts have been handed down to us by Michael Grove, one of the pioneers of Buffalo Valley, who died in 1827.[29]

Late in the fall of 1800, after the first snowfall, while out with one of his neighbors, Michael McClister, looking for wolf tracks, he noticed three buffalo, a bull, a cow and a calf, at the edge of a wood in one of his clearings. This clearing is a short distance south of the Kelly home. McClister fired, killing the calf, but the bull and cow escaped into the forest. This pair, which was of enormous size, was noticed from time to time in the neighborhood but managed to elude their pursuers. It seemed as if fate was preserving this, the last of the bison in Pennsylvania, to fall to the unerring bullet of the intrepid Colonel.

On the morning of January 19, 1801, Kelly was riding horseback on his way to the mill, mounted on "Brandywine," his old charger of the Revolution. It was a misty morning, and had not his horse snorted, he would have ridden squarely into a mammoth buffalo bull which completely blocked the narrow crossroads. Kelly dismounted from his horse and, taking leisurely aim, shot the bison through the heart.

The spot where this buffalo was killed, which proved to be the last of its species shot in Pennsylvania in a wild state, as far as proved, became known as Buffalo Cross-Roads. The huge skull, nailed to a pitch-pine tree, was a familiar landmark for many years. About 1820, it was blown from the tree in a gale, being picked up by one of the Kleckner children, relatives of the Kellys, and for half a century reposed in the garret of the

---

29. Michael Grove (1757-1827) served in the Pennsylvania Militia in the Revolutionary War. He is buried at Dreisbach United Church of Christ Cemetery, Lewisburg, Pennsylvania. He was a brother of the legendary Peter Grove, buried at Dunnstown Cemetery near Lock Haven, the protagonist of Herbert E. Stover's novel Song of the Susquehanna. How did Shoemaker get this tale from Michael Grove? There is no recorded source of Michael Grove's recollections.

GRAVE OF COL. JOHN KELLY,
In New Cemetery at Lewisburg.
(From photo by J. Herbert Walker.)

COL. KELLY HOMESTEAD.

Kleckner homestead in the vicinity of Buffalo Cross-Roads. When the mansion was remodeled some years ago, a careless house cleaner threw the horns into a basket of trash, and they were burned in a bonfire in the yard before their value was ascertained.

A slightly different version, from the lips of a Dr. Beck, is recorded in Professor Allen's *History of the American Bison,* page 485. The buffalo cow, which escaped McClister and Colonel Kelly in 1800, ultimately took refuge in the "tight end" of Buffalo Valley. There in the wilderness, it defied its pursuers for several years. Jonas J. Barnett,[30] aged 77 years, a splendid old gentleman residing at Weikert, Union County, informed the writer that his great uncle, Jacob Weikert, who settled on the site of the town bearing his name in 1800, went after this buffalo repeatedly, at last driving it out of the valley in the direction of Lewistown. Thus, the ultimate fate of the really *last* buffalo in Pennsylvania is unknown, unless later research in Mifflin County will bring it to light. A buffalo is said to have been killed on Buffalo Run, Centre County (near Hunter's Park). This might have been the same animal.

The career of Jacob Weikert reads like a romance. He was a native of Berks County, but preferring life in the unsettled regions, moved into the "narrow point" of Buffalo Valley. For seven years, he was unable to keep hogs on his place, owing to the depredations of panthers. All told, he probably killed over one thousand panthers, wolves, and bears, as well as countless deer and other game.

The Kelly homestead was remodeled in 1914. The giant open fireplaces where the old pioneer sat on winter evenings and told Indian and hunting stories were torn away, and the attic stripped of relics. It is said that the horns of several buffalo killed by Colonel Kelly prior to 1800 hung there for many years, but the writer, who visited the spot while the remodeling was in progress, accompanied by Mr. S. N. Rhoads, the Philadelphia naturalist, could not learn if they had been destroyed or lost. As few horns were preserved as trophies by the old timers, it was an unsentimental age; it would be unusual if these priceless souvenirs had been kept.

In the field east of the Kelly mansion is the grave of an Indian who came very near to putting an end to the Colonel's life. Years after the

---

30. Jonas J. Barnett (1838-1924) is buried at Hironimus Union Cemetery, Weikert, Union County, Pennsylvania.

Revolution, when Kelly was seated one fine June evening on his porch, he noticed something stir behind a large gum tree in his pasture-lot. As he never moved without his trusted rifle, he lifted it into position quickly, in time to let fly a ball at the head of an Indian as he poked it out for a moment from behind the tree. Before the savage could discharge his firearm, he was a dead Indian. Not wishing to terrify his women folks, Kelly strode down to the pasture and, with the aid of a manure-fork, buried the Indian, whom he recognized as Bull Head,[31] so named on account of his broad skull, and a native who cherished an old grudge against him.

One Christmas day, a few years later, when Colonel Kelly's grandchildren and great-grandchildren were playing in the yard, a hunting dog ran up with the Indian's skull in its mouth. There was great excitement for a time, to be sure. Explanations being necessary, the old Indian fighter related the episode to his family circle that evening as they were gathered around the inglenook.

Colonel Kelly was fond of young people, and until within four years of his death was known as the most accomplished dancer in Buffalo Valley. He died on February 18, 1832, aged 88 years. His remains rest under a handsome monument in the picturesque New Cemetery at Lewisburg. His grave has been a favorite shrine for lovers of history and sport, and for years it was pointed out to visitors by the late lamented sexton of the cemetery, Captain W. L. Donachy.[32]

As far as is known, no portrait of Colonel Kelly exists. His descendants aver that, like William Penn, the mighty buffalo hunter steadfastly refused to have his portrait painted. There is a rumor, however, that a traveling German artist sketched him unawares at the request of one of his sons. There are some persons who claim to have seen this likeness, and they say that it shows a man strikingly like George Washington in contour of features. Such a portrait, if in existence now, would be of priceless value, and diligent search should be made for it, and it should be deposited in the State Museum at Harrisburg.

---

31. Bull Head was a well-known chief in the West, circa 1895. Shoemaker may have borrowed the name.
32. William L. Donachy (1843-1915) was a Civil War veteran buried at Lewisburg.

VI.

RE-INTRODUCTION

FOR nearly half a century, Pennsylvania enjoyed the melancholy distinction of being the leading tanning ground for western buffalo hides. From about 1845 to 1885, it is estimated that one million bison hides were tanned in this state, mostly at the big tannery at Wilcox, Elk County. Many hides were sent there to be tanned and sold, in consequence of which they became a drag on the local market. They were sold to neighboring lumbermen and farmers at $20 per bale, a bale containing 12 hides. There are still a few of these hides to be picked up about Wilcox, those in good condition bringing never less than $50 apiece.

All through Pennsylvania, buffalo robes were familiar sights in farmhouses, in livery stables, and on sleighs, until very recently. Now they are scarce, except perhaps in Snyder County. The writer has a magnificent robe purchased from the estate of the late Cornelius Cromley,[33] of

---

33. Cornelius Cromley lived from 1839 to 1909 and is buried at McElhattan.

Clinton County, who had bought it in 1880 from John Wanamaker of Philadelphia at the price of $3.50. But the reintroduction of the buffalo in living form will be more interesting to the readers of these pages.

Shortly after the Civil War, a number of bison were shipped to this state, butchered and served at barbecues. One of the most famous of these was when a Kansas buffalo weighing a ton was slaughtered at Reading, at a big political barbecue during the Tilden campaign of 1876.[34] A live buffalo calf was shipped from Nebraska to Abe Sheesley of Jersey Shore in 1879, and for a year or two, it made a gentle and affectionate pet. During the rutting season in the animal's third year, he jumped fences, butted down small buildings, and chased dogs and children, making himself generally obnoxious.

Finally, the animal was chained in a stable, where he was kept for several years. He was mated with several cows of the domestic variety, and his offspring were said to be handsome creatures. Unfortunately, they had little respect for fences or enclosures and generally had to be killed when two or three years old. Mr. Sheesley became tired of his unmanageable pet and had him butchered. The animal weighed, dressed, a ton, and the good people of Jersey Shore and Chatham's Run besieged butcher W. H. Schwer's traveling market wagon to taste the flesh of the late monarch of the plains. The horns adorned the Sheesley home for many years.

In Colonel John G. Millais' interesting book *British Deer and Their Horns* is an amusing account of a herd of buffalo exported from the United States to Scotland by Sir William Stewart, who served at the Battle of Waterloo. It is as follows: "Sir William was one of the first men 'out west,' and his life was a complete romance. Certain aspersions were cast on his pluck after Waterloo, and to show that they were false, he went out to the Rocky Mountains and lived amongst the Sioux for five years. There, he became a first-class bandit, but displayed such courage that they made him a chief.

"Wearying of his wild life, he returned to Murthly, bringing with him, however, almost a dozen of his pals amongst the Sioux, and a herd of buffalo. The latter he lodged in a beautiful park at Rohallion, surrounding it with a stone wall seven feet high, and with a wire fence on top of that. If my reader is a lover of *Punch,* which he is pretty sure to

---

34. New York Governor Samuel Tilden ran for President as a Democrat.

JONAS J. BARNETT,
grand-nephew of Jacob Weikert, one of the last
hunters of bison in Pennsylvania.

LOOKING DOWN THE BUFFALO PATH.
(Union County.)

be, he will recollect a drawing, by John Leech, of Mr. Briggs being taken through Buffalo Park by his friend. That friend was my father (Sir John E. Millais), and Mr. Briggs was, of course, Leech himself. I have often heard the story of that day amongst the buffalo. By and by, the buffaloes died off or were killed, and the last old bull broke out of the park somehow, and, meeting the mail coach going north, proceeded to knock the stuffin' out of the horses. But there was an unfeeling man on the coach who had a rifle and no sense of humor, so the last of the Scotch buffaloes had to go."

In various Zoological Gardens in Pennsylvania, buffalo have thrived remarkably well. The Philadelphia Zoo in Fairmount Park, which was founded in 1859 and opened to the public in 1874, has usually maintained a group of about a dozen head. In 1886, the Gardens sold an adult bull and cow to Colonel W. F. Cody (Buffalo Bill) for $300. At the Zoo in Highland Park, Pittsburgh, at present, there are two young female bison, purchased last year from Earl E. Bennett, Newport, New Hampshire. A male from Yellowstone Park is shortly to be added to this herd. At the Reading Zoo, there are no buffalo at present, but as soon as appropriation can be secured for their maintenance, a cow and bull will be shipped there from Yellowstone Park. In several private parks in different parts of the state, buffalo are kept, notably at the magnificent game preserve of Colonel Harry C. Trexler,[35] "The Cement King," near Allentown, where there is a herd of 20 of these noble brutes.

---

35. Harry Clay Trexler (1854-1933) earned the rank of General from his service with the quartermaster corps of the National Guard during the Spanish-American War and World War I. In 1890, he took over his family lumber business in Allentown, Pennsylvania, and turned it into one of the largest lumber companies on the East Coast. In 1897, along with two business associates, he formed the Lehigh Portland Cement Company. It would become the largest maker of cement in the United States. In 1905, he and a business partner took over the Lehigh Valley Traction Company and renamed it the Lehigh Valley Transit Company. Lines were expanded to connect all the cities in the Lehigh Valley, and there was even a rail line connecting Allentown and Philadelphia. He also played a prominent role in the creation of the Pennsylvania Power & Light Company and the Bell Telephone. He created West Park in Allentown; established Romper Day in Allentown on August 28, 1914, an event which has been held annually ever since; he founded the Trexler Game Preserve and brought buffalo from the west when they were in danger of extinction. The buffalo have thrived there to this day; he donated fish hatchery land to the city of Allentown, which eventually became Lehigh Parkway. He died from injuries received in an auto accident, but his will established a $10 million Trexler Trust to be put in place upon the death of his wife. When his wife died on December 20, 1934, the amount of the Trexler Trust increased to $12 million. The Harry Trexler Trust has now distributed nearly $85 million to the Allentown Park System and other charitable organizations over its 70-plus years of existence. His country estate was converted into Trexler Memorial Park. A bronze statue of General Trexler on his horse "Jack O' Diamonds" presides over the grounds.

As game animals, the buffalo will probably never be reintroduced in Pennsylvania, although their docile habits and hardy natures would make them adaptable in some of the wilder sections of the state. Perhaps with the spread of the hoof-and-mouth disease and bovine tuberculosis, a sentiment in favor of full-bred or half-bred bison to replace the present breeds of domestic cattle will be instituted. The bison are not subject to these diseases and would flourish on the abandoned slashings and bare mountain tops in the Pennsylvania wilds. Berks County farmers have been talking about starting to pasture herds of steers on the Blue Mountains, but buffaloes would be heartier and more remunerative.

Between 1870 and 1875, it is conservatively estimated that one million wild buffalo were killed annually in the West. Most of these were wasted, and their hides frittered away for paltry sums. May the day come when a like number of tame bison are butchered in Pennsylvania, to our citizens' advantage.

Albert Gallatin, the financier of New Geneva, Fayette County, wrote considerably about the domestication of the bison, which he believed was entirely feasible. He said that many had been kept and successfully bred by farmers south of Mason and Dixon's Line. At one period, for eight months, he lived off buffalo meat and enjoyed it. He also believed in the practicability of crossing bison with domestic cattle and mentioned a farmer living on the Monongahela River who owned a large buffalo bull, which he allowed to roam at large with his farm cattle, and which was "no more dangerous to man than any bull of the common species." Mr. J. W. Cunningham, of Erie, formerly of Howard County, Nebraska, successfully experimented with crossing bison and domestic cattle.

VII.

DANIEL OTT

GRANDSON of George Ott, one of the original buffalo hunters of central Pennsylvania and himself slayer of many hundreds of bison on the plains of the Great West, Daniel Ott of Selinsgrove, Snyder County, is one of the historically noteworthy personages of the Keystone State. In company with Honorable George W. Wagenseller,[36] editor of the *Middleburg Post*, and J. Herbert Walker, associate editor of the *Lewisburg Journal*, the writer recently visited the venerable nimrod at his cozy home on the outskirts of the quaint old town of Selin's Grove.

Nimble and mentally alert despite his 95 years, the old hunter, who is still a handsome man and has the aquiline nose and tight drawn lips which are usually signs of character, greeted his guests cordially, and unfolded to them the marvelous story of his life. Frequently during the narrative, he

---

36. George Washington Wagenseller lived from 1868 to 1951.

told jokes which convulsed his hearers, and his fine amber colored eyes, as clear as those of the poet Keats, were alive with keenness and humor. Daniel Ott was born in Selinsgrove on May 27, 1820, being the son of Daniel Ott, Sr. (1784–1852) and grandson of George Ott (1745–1814), one of the original pioneers on the Karoondinha, now known as Penn's Creek.[37] George Ott, who was a native of Chester County, took up 400 acres of wild land in what is now Snyder County in 1796, when that region still abounded with wild beasts and roving Indians. In Daniel Ott's own words, let him describe his thrilling life's pilgrimage.

"I was born in the house where I now reside and am of Dutch and English ancestry. My father and grandfather, the pioneers, were not hunters in the modern meaning of the word, as the game came up to their doors to be shot. Buffaloes and other game were plentiful north of Jack's Mountain when they came into this country. When I was a boy, wolves were numerous, and at night we could hear them howling from the summits of the Spangenberg and the Mahanoy Mountain, and they even howled from the top of the Blue Hill at the good people across the river at Sunbury. In those early days, I killed and helped to kill many wolves; they were grayer in color than the ones I afterwards met with in the west.

"I hunted all kinds of game in Pennsylvania and was a fisherman as well. I have killed too many deer to count them, the first when I was a mere boy, and the last, when I was eighty years old, I brought down on Jack's Mountain. The horns of that stag I still have. I was a good-sized boy when Halley's comet appeared in 1834; I saw it again 76 years later in 1910. I saw the famous falling stars one night in 1835. In the White Mountains, back of Jack's Mountain, I once killed a half-deer, half-elk. It had one horn like a deer and the other like an elk, and dressed over 200 pounds.

"In addition to wolves and deer, I killed many bears, catamounts, and wild cats. On two occasions, I came face-to-face with big panthers, but they eluded me. The flights of wild pigeons, which used to come to Selin's Grove, darkened the sun. I have trapped 1300 wild pigeons in one

---

37. Daniel Ott served in the Civil War, a Private in Co. I, 49th Reg. P.V.I, from March 1864 to July 1865. He died on July 19, 1916, at Penns, Snyder County, Pennsylvania. He was 91 years, 1 month, and 22 days old. Daniel was buried at the south section of Union Cemetery on July 22nd. Daniel is mentioned in several of Henry Shoemaker's books of wildlife as one of Snyder County's greatest deer hunters.

DANIEL OTT,
Born May 27, 1820, a Pennsylvanian who has killed
many buffaloes in the West.

day. The nesting grounds of the wild pigeons were arranged with military precision. Sometimes they were in the shape of squares, other times circles. The trees marking the boundary had no nests on the branches outside the line. It was strange to see trees full of nests on one side and with none on the other.

"I remember when the Susquehanna River and Penn's Creek were alive with shad. That was before the days of pollution from the tanneries and paper mills. I have caught 500 shad at a single haul. When I was a boy, there were still a few Indians in this country; they used to travel along the riverbank and rest under the big trees in the shade.

"In 1841, I came to the conclusion that I would like to visit the big game regions of the West. As there were no railroads, and stage travelling was expensive, I resolved to set out on foot. The stages and freighters which crossed the Alleghenies were drawn by the now extinct Conestoga horses. The Conestoga horses were better looking than any draft animals of the present day. They were chunky built, with full necks, short heads, and fine, full eyes. Although they would weigh on average 1200 pounds, they did not stand over 15:2 hands. They had particularly good hoofs, much like those of the fast-traveling Percherons.

"I walked from Selinsgrove to the Big Valley, to Bedford, to Wheeling, to Columbus, to Dayton, across the Black Swamp on the Corduroy Road to Indianapolis. The Indiana capital then consisted of a few wooden houses and was surrounded by magnificent hardwood forests. Deer, wolves, and coyotes abounded. Raccoons were a nuisance to the settlers. One night, with several friends, I was out hunting 'coons along the White River, when we became lost in the woods. We got in a hollow buttonwood tree for safety, and none too soon, for we were surrounded by a yelping pack of coyotes which kept us prisoners until daylight. West of Indianapolis was a wild prairie country, where wolves roamed, and where there were millions of prairie chickens.

"I decided to walk to Springfield, which I found to be a small village like Indianapolis. Abe Lincoln was there, carelessly dressed and ungainly, a familiar figure about the streets. The inaccessibility of the country between Indianapolis and Springfield led me to say to my companion, 'Nobody will ever live in this region; it is too hard to reach with supplies.'

West of Springfield in Missouri, there were still great herds of buffalo and antelopes.

"I decided to walk to Chicago, through the wild prairie region. Each night, I trusted to reach some settler's cabin, as I hated to sleep out on the plains on account of the wolves and coyotes. I saw coyotes and prairie chickens on the outskirts of the Windy City. When I got there, I found only a single line of frame houses, one story and one story and a half high, facing the Lake on what is now Michigan Avenue. It was a dreary place, so I struck out for Indianapolis, which town I liked very much.

"I travelled through the West for a number of years; my experiences would fill a book, meeting Indians, traders, and hunters, and killing much game myself. In the height of the buffalo excitement, I organized a hide hunting expedition to go to the Panhandle district in Texas, where herds of hundreds of thousands of these noble animals roamed the plains. Our outfit left Dodge City, which is in Ford County, Kansas, and headed south. Dodge City was, in those days (in the early seventies), one of the headquarters of the buffalo trade. Piles of hides a hundred feet high were stacked in all parts of the town. Only the choicest hides, those from the cows and heifers, were used for robes; the tough hides of the old bulls went for belting.

"We were soon in the buffalo country, as the plains were covered with the carcasses of dead bison. Some were killed for 'fun' and never even skinned, others had their hides stripped off and left for the wolves. We could see where they had been killed in former years, as where they laid the buffalo grass died, and weeds sprang up, and the skulls and horns were mournful relics of man's wastefulness. When we camped at night, bands of noisy coyotes came close to our camps, and I shot many of them. When they barked, the large gray wolves often answered them, but the big wolves were shy, and we seldom saw them.

"In Indian Territory, now Oklahoma, near the Cimarron River, I saw a herd of wild horses. They were the most beautiful animals I have ever seen. They were blood bays, with black manes and tails. Their heads were small, their ears short, and they stood higher in front than in back. My companions wanted to shoot them, but I told them not to, as it would be a shame to kill such handsome creatures for no good purpose.

Meanwhile, the grand stallion, which led them, sighted us, snorted, which was the signal to the herd to make off, and they started away in single file at a trot.

"Buffaloes always run with the wind; nothing can turn them. The aim of the hunters is to get them off the wind, approach close, and shoot them. The first herd we surprised was given the signal by a big bull and started for us. We waved our hats as they came near, but they would not turn from their course. Fearing that they would run us down, we took to our heels. As the big brutes passed, my companion, George Harrison, fired a dozen shots into them. I asked him why he fired at them when he knew he could not kill them. He said he did it because they 'kicked so funny' when hit. I told him that the buffaloes so wounded would die a lingering death on the prairie, would be eaten by the wolves, and their hides wasted. Harrison said he had never thought of that before.

"Ever after I made it the rule of our expedition only to kill such buffaloes as we could use the hides, or in self-defense. As for arms, our expedition used Sharp's Needle Guns, which were calculated to carry a one-ounce ball 1,000 yards. Some hunters used breech-loading U. S. Muskets or Winchester rifles. In the fall of the year, when we did most of our killing, the small family groups of buffalo were beginning to come together in the vast herds that assembled during the winter months for mutual protection. In the summer, they separated into parties of about one hundred animals each, and slept, pastured, and travelled in such groups. Every party of buffalo had their watchers, which gave the signal of the approach of human or animal foes, while the others rested or munched the sweet buffalo grass.

"We stalked our buffaloes, crawling along through the grass until we got near them; then before we could be seen, as we approached 'off' the wind, we selected our victims and fired. We always carried five skinners to one killer, as it took a great amount of care to scrape all the fat off the hides, and unless this was done, they were hard to keep. The air in the buffalo country was so dry that no odor emanated from the carcasses which strewed the plains, looking in the distance like hillocks. At nightfall, the hordes of wolves drawn to the neighborhood by the food, feasted and fought over the remains.

"At our camps, we made our fires with buffalo chips, which furnished a clean and very hot fire. We usually selected a hole in the turf made by the buffalo's hoofs, laid a sheet of newspaper at the bottom of the hole, and placed the chips on top. Then we touched a match to the paper, soon having a splendid blaze.

"The size of the buffalo bulls was enormous. They would average over a thousand pounds, and some weighed close to a ton. They were covered with layer after layer of thick fat. When we collected as many hides as we could transport on our wagons, we started for Dodge City, where we sold the hides at an average price of two dollars apiece. We generally took a ton of selected buffalo meat with us on our northern journeys. On our trips, we met many Indians: Comanches, Cherokees, Arapahos, Cheyenne, and so on. They all chided us for our wholesale killing of what they called their cattle. They were particularly upset over the white man's wasteful methods of killing the bison. They only killed what they absolutely needed, they maintained.

"Many persons have wondered why the United States Government made no effort to stop the killing of the buffalo on Uncle Sam's Farm, as the boundless plains were called. The Government in those days could not control the Indians; it had its hands full there. Consequently, a 'side issue' like game protection was out of the question. But it was a great pity, as the buffaloes might have become the cattle of the West, as they were heartier than any of the varieties brought there. I saw many long-horned Texas steers. They were wonderful animals, and adapted themselves to local conditions; it is a pity their stock has been allowed to die out.

"On the plains with the buffalo were vast herds of prong-horned antelopes. We killed many of these as their flesh was good and their hides were of some value. Many hunters killed them for sport, firing into the herds at random, and letting the poor creatures die lingering deaths. I am glad I hunted buffalo, and while I killed a great number, I do not have it on my soul that I killed a single one for sport. All I killed were used as much as possible. I cut out the best meat and saved and sold the hides. I tried to induce the other hunters to be less wasteful, and I think I had influence with some of them.

"I had an experience that I would not exchange with anyone in the world. As I sit here, looking down the river to the towering Mahanoy, I think about how things have changed. All the big timber that covered the Mahanoy Range is gone, and there is no game here anymore worthy of name. There are few ducks in the river, no flights of wild pigeons darken the sun, an Indian is a curiosity, rafting is done, there are no more arks, gone is the canal which I saw built, everything is becoming tame and commonplace.

"I have lived a long while—ninety-five years, but I would like to live longer in this beautiful world if I can retain my faculties and not become a burden to my family. I can read without glasses, have my own teeth and have a good head of hair. Last week, I chopped down a dead apple tree; you can see the pile of stove wood I made from it if you look out the back door. Yesterday I butchered a big hog and shot the head off a rooster. Up to a few years ago, I often walked to Middleburg, ten miles; I take some pretty long walks still. Lots of people come to see me, and I have a loving, considerate family.[38]

"Over in the next room, I keep my hunting trophies. In the evenings when the wind howls about the old house, I go in and sit beside them, the heads and horns of buffalo, deer and antelopes I shot in the old days. Then I feel myself back in the wilds of Jack's Mountain, or in Clearfield County, or in the endless plains. I hear the tramp of the bison herds, the shouts of the victorious hunters, or maybe the blood-curdling cry of the panther.

"Then my mind goes back still further, and I hear my father tell of how his father took part in the hunting of the last herds of bison in old Pennsylvania, of Indian massacres, of pioneer hardships; and I feel proud to be the scion of such sturdy stock. Yes, indeed, I have much to be thankful for in this grand world; I have lived, I have struggled, I have harmed no one, in my advanced age, I am at peace, I am content."

---

38. The rest of this account appears to be added by Shoemaker and not the words of Ott.

INDEX

Allen, Joel Asaph, 2, 14, 28
Allentown, Pennsylvania, 34
Arbogast, Peter, 21
Ashe, Thomas, 6, 14–16

Bald Eagle Mountains, 7
Barnett, Jonas J., 28, 32
Beck, Dr., 28
Bedford, Pennsylvania, 39
Benfer, George, 21
Bennett, Earl E., 34
Bergstresser, Flavel, 17–18
Bergstresser, Katie, 19
Bergstresser, Martin, 17–20, 22
Big Buffalo Creek, 14
Big Flats, 21
Big Valley, 39
Black Gap, 23
Boonestiel's Tongue, 21
Bronx Zoo, v
Buffalo Creek, 6, 22, 24
Buffalo Cross-Roads, 25, 28
Buffalo Crossroads Presbyterian Cemetery, 19
Buffalo Field, 21
Buffalo Gap, 13
Buffalo Mountains, 6
Buffalo, New York, 12
Buffalo Park, 33
Buffalo Path, 6, 33
Buffalo Path Run, 13
Buffalo Valley, 6, 17, 24–25, 28–29
Bull Head, xi, 29

Castanea Gap, 8
Chatham's Run, 31

Chicago, Illinois, 40
Cimarron River, 40
Clarion, Pennsylvania, 14–16
Clearfield, Pennsylvania, 6–7, 43
Cody, William F. Cody (aka Buffalo Bill), 34
Cromley, Cornelius, 30
Columbus, Ohio, 39
Council Kup, 21
Cunningham, J. W., 35

Dayton, Ohio, 39
Dodge City, Kansas, 40
Donachy, William L., 29
Doran, William, 20
Dressler, Adam, 21
Dyce, John Q., 18

Engle, Daniel, 23
Ettwein, John, 7
Everhart, George, 20

Farnsworth, Jonathan, 21
Filson, John, 16
Five Springs, Pennsylvania, 5
Fisher, Christian, 20
Fisher, Peter, 20
French Creek, 14
Fryer, Gottfried, 20
Fryer, Jacob, 20

Gallatin, Albert, 2, 35
Gilfillan, Betsey, ii
Good, George, 21
Great Island, 7–8, 10
Gregg Township, 12

INDEX

Grove, Michael, xi, 25
Grove, Peter, xi, 25

Hager, John, 20
Haldeman's Island, 15
Harrison, George, 41
Hartman, John, 21
Henry Run Gap, 8, 11, 14
Highland Park, 34
Hittardantive, John, 21
Hornaday, William Temple Hornaday, v–vi, 2
Hummel, John, 21
Hyloshotkee, 5–6

Indianapolis, Indiana, 39–40

Jack's Mountain, 37, 43
Jarrett, Jacob, 21
Jersey Shore, Pennsylvania, 31

Kalm, Peter, 1
Kammerdiner Run, 8
Karoondinha Creek, xi, 37
Kelly, John, xi, 23–29
Kelly Township, 25
Kessler, George, 21
Kleckner Family, 17, 25, 28
Kreigbaum, John, 21

Lauder, Henry, 21
Le Boeuf Lake, 14
Le Boeuf, Pennsylvania, 14
Leech, John, 34
Lehr, Harry, 21
Lewisburg, Pennsylvania, 26, 29
Lewistown, Pennsylvania, 28
Linnaeus, Carl, 1
Logan the Orator, 5
Long, Jacob, 20

Mahanoy Mountain, 37
Mahanoy Range, 43
McClellan, Samuel, xi, 19–21
McClister, Michael, 25, 28

McElhattan Pass, 8
McElhattan, Pennsylvania, 5, 8, 30
McElhattan Run, 8
Michael, George, 20
Middle Creek Valley, 6–7, 10, 14, 18, 22
Middleburg, Pennsylvania, 36, 43
Middleswarth, John, 21
Millais, John G., 31, 34
Miller, Solomon, 21
Monongahela River, 35
Mucklehenny, Dennis, 20

New Geneva, Pennsylvania, 35
Newport, New Hampshire, 34

Oil Creek, 14
Old Logan, 19–20
Ott, Daniel, 36, 39–43
Ott, George, 19, 36–37

Pardee, Ario, 4
Pauling, Joseph, 21
Penn, William, 1, 29
Penn's Creek, 7, 37, 39
Philadelphia Zoo, 34
Pittsburgh, Pennsylvania, 22, 34

Quiggle, Catherine Strayer, ii
Quiggle Cemetery, ii
Quiggle, George Sr., ii
Quiggle, Jacob S., ii, 6
Quiggle, James W., ii
Quiggle, Philip (aka Philip Quigley), ii, 6–7, 9, 14
Quiggle Springs, 5

Reading Zoo, 34
Rhoads, Francis, 21
Rhoads, Samuel Nicholson, 2, 14, 28
Roan, Flavel, 17
Roan, John, 17

Schnable, George, 20
Schoepff, Johann David, 1, 22
Schwer, W. H., 31

Selinsgrove, Pennsylvania, 25, 37, 39
Sharp's Needle Guns, 41
Seven Mountains, 11–12, 18, 22
Sheesley, Abe, 31
Snyder, Emmanuel, 20
Sourkill, Abraham, 20
Spangenberg Mountain, 37
Spring Run, 8
Springfield, Illinois, 39–40
Stony Creek, 15
Stuck, Jacob, 20
Sugar Valley, 6
Sunbury, Pennsylvania, 2, 37
Susquehanna River, 2, 7, 39
Susquehanna Valley, xi
Swineford, Albert, 21
Swineford, George, 21
Swineford, John, 21

Tilden, Samuel, 31
Trexler, Harry C., 34
Troup, Moses, 21
Troup, Peter, 21
Troxelville, Pennsylvania, 22

Wagenseller, George Washington, 36
Walker, J. Herbert, 25, 36
Wanamaker, John, 31
Washington, George, 29
Waterford, Pennsylvania, 14
Weikert, Jacob, 28, 32
Weikert, Pennsylvania, 21
Weirick, George, 21
Weiser, Conrad Jr., 21
West Branch, 6, 10, 12, 18, 22
Wheeling, West Virginia, 39
White Deer Valley, 4, 6, 11
White Mountains, 6, 17, 21, 37
Wickersham, George, 21
Wilcox, Pennsylvania, 30
Winchester rifles, 41
Wren, Mary, 4

Yellowstone Park, 34
Young, John, 20

Zimmerman, David A., 4
Zimmerman, Jacob Wren, 4

www.ingramcontent.com/pod-product-compliance
Lightning Source LLC
Chambersburg PA
CBHW011802040426
42449CB00016B/3466